RELATIONSHIPS IN NATURE

by KATHY KINSNER

Table of Contents

Introduction		2
Chapter 1	Predator and Prey: Hunters and Hunted	4
Chapter 2	Mutualism: Animal Partners	16
Chapter 3	Parasitism: Uninvited Guests	21
Chapter 4	The Human Connection	24
Conclusion		30
Glossary		31
Index		32

Introduction

A cheetah leaps into action. It's in hot pursuit of a gazelle—its dinner. A brightly colored clown fish darts among the tentacles of a sea anemone. It's seeking protection to avoid being eaten. A mosquito lands on a person's arm. It's ready for a meal of human blood.

Animals depend upon each other in many ways to survive. In this book, you'll explore three main types of relationships among animals. In Chapter 1, you'll learn about the predator-prey relationships of the hunters and the hunted. Chapter 2 will introduce you to special relationships in which both **species** benefit. Chapter 3 will let you check out animal relationships in which one benefits and the other is usually harmed.

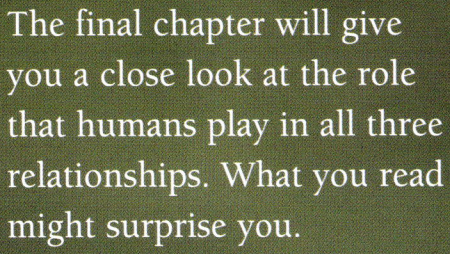

The final chapter will give you a close look at the role that humans play in all three relationships. What you read might surprise you.

As you make your way through the book, you'll read interesting tidbits about a variety of unusual animals. So, if you're ready to meet flying frogs, lizards that walk on water, and snakes that play dead, read on.

CHAPTER 1

Predator and Prey:
Hunters and Hunted

Animals that hunt for their food are called **predators**. The animals they eat are called **prey**. It's possible for an animal to be both predator and prey. For example, a rattlesnake is a predator when it preys on a lizard. But when a hawk eats a rattlesnake, the hawk is the predator and the rattlesnake is now the prey.

In a predator–prey relationship, who is in control—the predator or the prey? Predators kill their prey for food in order to survive. So, on the surface it seems clear that the predator is always in control. However, a closer look at the predator–prey relationship between the lynx and snowshoe hare shows that the answer is not so clear after all.

hawk as predator

rattlesnake as prey

rattlesnake as predator

lizard as prey

4

Lynx and Snowshoe Hare

- When the snowshoe hare population is high, the lynx predator has no problem finding enough to eat.

- If the lynx overhunts the hare, it must find a different prey in order to survive.

- In the winter, the hare's food supply decreases. As a result, the hare population starts to decrease also. The lynx must find different prey in order to survive.

- If the lynx cannot find enough new prey, the lynx population starts to drop.

- With fewer lynx predators, the snowshoe hare population starts to increase again.

A lynx pursues a hare—its future meal.

CHAPTER 1

Snail Kite and Apple Snail

A snail kite and an apple snail are another example of a predator–prey relationship. The snail kite is a medium-sized hawk that lives in the Florida Everglades. It eats one food—the apple snail—and very little else.

The snail kite is an expert at capturing the apple snail. It swoops down and snatches the apple snail out of the water with one foot. With luck, the snail kite doesn't even get its belly wet.

New construction in the Everglades has reduced the apple snail's **habitat**. Fewer places to live means fewer apple snails for the snail kite to eat. As a result, the snail kite was put on the list of endangered species. Their numbers are now increasing, thanks to efforts to protect them.

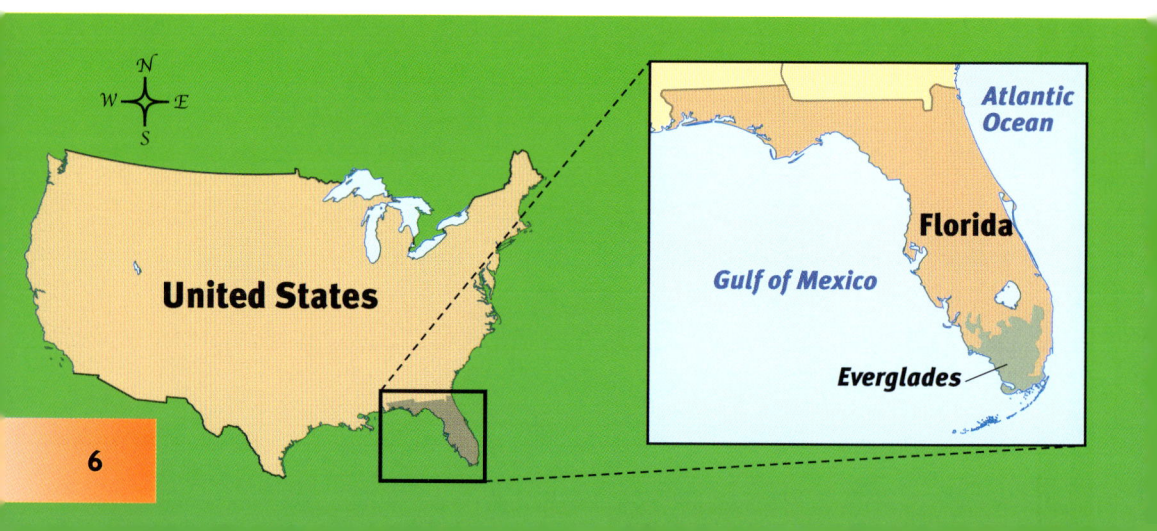

A snail kite holds an apple snail in its talons.

PREDATOR AND PREY: HUNTERS AND HUNTED

It's a FACT

The ways in which predators and prey are connected are not always obvious. Look at the diagram on this page. It shows how some of the animals that live in the Florida Everglades are connected. Alligators do not eat crayfish or the eggs of wading birds. But crayfish and eggs are important to the alligators' survival. Why? Because alligators might eat raccoons, and raccoons couldn't survive without crayfish or eggs to eat.

alligator

raccoon

crayfish

eggs of wading bird

CHAPTER 1

Look closely. Can you find the walking stick?

Predator Techniques and Prey Survival

Predators use many methods to capture their prey. Some predators are very fast and simply chase their victims. Others hide out and ambush, or make a surprise attack on, their prey. Still other predators hunt in packs. That way they can kill bigger prey than if they hunted alone.

Some prey have **adapted** to protect themselves. An insect called a walking stick looks like a twig. By blending in with its surroundings, walking sticks can sometimes fool the predators that hunt them. Some prey are brightly colored. This warns predators that they are poisonous and should not be eaten.

PREDATOR AND PREY: HUNTERS AND HUNTED

Some prey survive as a species because they have so many babies. Mice are prey to many different predators. But they survive as a species because one mouse may have ten litters a year. If each litter includes five to six babies, that's fifty to sixty new mice a year from just one mouse!

baby mice asleep in their nest

It's a FACT

Some predator animals use tools to get food. New Caledonian crows have been seen using leaves and twigs to dig out insects from hard-to-reach places. In a science lab, these birds have used even more sophisticated tools to capture their prey.

Scientists placed food at the bottom of a tall tube. Two New Caledonian crows named Betty and Abel had to get the food out of the tube. The scientists gave the crows two wires, one straight and one shaped like a hook. Each crow chose the hooked wire to snag the food.

Then Abel flew away with the hooked wire. Betty bent the straight wire into a hook and used it to get the food!

CHAPTER 1

10 Ways to Get a Meal

Here are ten ways predators are successful.

1. **Run, swim, or fly fast.** A cheetah can run more than 60 miles per hour. Its speed helps it catch prey, such as small antelope. But it can maintain its speed for only a few hundred yards.

cheetah

2. **Run, swim, or fly for a long time.** Wolves can run up to 35 miles per hour for only short distances. But they can trot at slower speeds for hours and tire out moose and other prey.

3. **Inject poison.** Cobras have poison glands connected to their fangs. When a cobra bites a mouse or other prey, it injects it with poison. The poison injures the prey so the cobra can eat it.

4. **Get a grip.** A hawk has sharp claws, called talons, perfect for nabbing fish, reptiles, and other prey.

wolf

5. **Hunt in a group.** Orcas (killer whales) work together to herd fish and other prey into small areas. Then they attack.

6. **Have good eyesight.** Eagles have excellent eyesight and can spot their prey from a mile away. Eagles can tell the difference between similar colors, making it easier to spot small animals, such as rabbits.

bald eagle

7. **Build a trap.** Many spiders cover their webs with sticky drops. The drops help to trap insects.

8. **Use tools.** The Egyptian vulture uses rocks to break ostrich eggs. The sea otter uses rocks to open clamshells. And the chimpanzee uses twigs to "fish" for termites.

9. **Be patient.** The polar bear waits by breaks in the ice, grabbing seals as they come up for air.

10. **Blend in with the scenery.** The praying mantis looks like the plants it sits on. Its prey, other insects, might not see the mantis until it is too late.

polar bear

CHAPTER 1

10 Ways to Avoid Being a Meal

Here are ten ways prey avoid being eaten.

1. **Be poisonous.** Porcupine fish have sharp spines and poisonous skin, making them deadly if swallowed.

2. **Blend in with the scenery.** The Kallima butterfly uses **camouflage** to blend into its surroundings. By pressing its wings together over its back and resting against a twig, the Kallima looks like a dead leaf and goes unnoticed.

3. **Use your armor.** The pangolin, or scaly anteater, is covered in sharp scales that act like armor. When threatened, it rolls up into a ball, protecting its belly.

4. **Run, swim, or fly away.** The basilisk lizard escapes predators by running across the water on its back legs. Eventually it slows down and swims away. The Costa Rican flying tree frog doesn't really fly. Its webbed feet help it glide through the air as it leaps from branch to branch.

5. **Play dead.** Many predators won't eat animals that are already dead. The hog-nosed snake plays dead by lying on its back with its mouth hanging open.

porcupine fish

basilisk lizard

PREDATOR AND PREY: HUNTERS AND HUNTED

6. **Taste bad.** The poison arrow frog's colorful skin warns predators that it's poisonous. If eaten, the frog will be bad-tasting. The hope is that the predator will spit out the frog and let it go.

7. **Spray something.** The Texas horned lizard squirts toxic blood from its eyes. Skunks lift their tails to squirt a bad-smelling liquid that stings predators' eyes.

8. **Bite, scratch, or kick.** A kangaroo bites, kicks, and uses its strong nails to defend itself.

9. **Lose it.** Some lizards escape even after being caught by the tail! The tail can break off in the predator's mouth, allowing the lizard to scurry away.

10. **Warn each other.** Prairie dogs bark to warn each other of danger. Then they disappear into burrows until it's safe to pop back up.

blue poison arrow frog

prairie dog

✓ Point

Reread
Reread and find five ways in which animals can be successful predators and five ways in which animals can avoid becoming prey.

CHAPTER 1

Scavengers

Some predators are also **scavengers**, animals that eat the bodies of dead animals. The spotted hyena of Africa is both a predator and a scavenger.

Usually, a hyena starts hunting and scavenging alone. Once it makes a kill or finds a dead animal, other hyenas join in the feast. A pack of hyenas is bold enough to chase a cheetah away from an animal it has just killed.

It's a FACT

Spotted hyenas are also called laughing hyenas because of their funny howl. It sounds like a person laughing hysterically.

PREDATOR AND PREY: HUNTERS AND HUNTED

A black vulture dines on the body of a dead animal.

Most vultures do not prey on live animals. They are scavengers that eat only the bodies of dead animals. Vultures have special skills and features that make them successful scavengers. They are strong fliers and have amazing eyesight. They can spot a dying animal from very far away! These scavengers are messy eaters. But with no feathers on their heads, they can keep at least that part of their bodies clean while dining!

It's a FACT

Dung beetles are not your typical scavengers. Instead of feasting on dead animals, these scavengers eat animal droppings. In fact, 16,000 dung beetles have cleaned up over three pounds (1.5 kilograms) of elephant dung in just two hours!

Some female dung beetles roll pieces of dung into a ball. They then roll the ball away from the rest of the dung and bury it. The females either eat the dung ball or lay their eggs on it. When the eggs hatch, the young beetles eat the dung.

CHAPTER 2

Mutualism
Animal Partners

Some animals have special partnerships in which both sides benefit. **Mutualism** (MYOO-chuh-wuh-lih-zum) is the word used to describe these relationships.

Clown Fish and Sea Anemone

The partnership between the clown fish and the sea anemone (uh-NEH-muh-nee) is an example of mutualism. The colors of the clown fish make it easy prey for bigger fish. Clown fish are also very slow swimmers. To protect themselves, they live in small groups among sea anemones.

The sea anemone is an animal that looks a lot like a plant. Its mouth is surrounded by tentacles. These tentacles have stinging cells that spit out poison. Clown fish are immune to the sea anemone's sting. They can swim among the tentacles unharmed. If a predator gets too close to the clown fish, it will be stung by the sea anemone's tentacles.

A clown fish uses a sea anemone to protect itself.

It's clear how the clown fish benefits from this relationship. But what about the sea anemone? Does it get anything in return? Yes—it gets a meal! Once a predator has been stung by the anemone, the predator becomes paralyzed. The sea anemone uses its tentacles to pull the predator into its mouth. When the sea anemone has had its fill, the clown fish benefits again. It gets to eat the scraps that the sea anemone leaves behind.

a sea anemone eating a crab

CHAPTER 2

Wrasse and Big Fish

The relationship that a small fish called a wrasse (RAS) has with a bigger fish, such as a grouper, is another example of mutualism. The wrasse does a little "dance" in front of a big fish to let it know it should slow down and open its mouth. The wrasse then swims in and cleans the big fish's mouth and gills! The wrasse gets a meal. The bigger fish gets a cleaner mouth—which means less chance of disease.

Honey Badger and Honeyguide

The honey badger and the honeyguide are another example of mutualism. Honey is one of the honey badger's favorite foods. A bird called a honeyguide leads the honey badger to a beehive. The honey badger tears open the hive with its long front claws. Inside is a treat for two—honey for the badger, and beeswax and grubs for the honeyguide.

a grouper and a wrasse

MUTUALISM: ANIMAL PARTNERS

Look closely. Can you see the tiny green aphids?

Ant and Aphid

The ant and the aphid are insect partners. Aphids suck liquid from the stems, leaves, and roots of plants. Then aphids produce and secrete, or ooze, a sweet substance called honeydew. When an ant wants a drink, it uses its antennae to tap an aphid. Out comes a drop of honeydew.

How does the aphid benefit? Some ants protect aphids from predators. One kind of ant stores aphids' eggs underground during the winter. When the weather warms up, the ants bring the eggs out to hatch.

Oxpecker and Water Buffalo

An oxpecker is a bird that spends its days traveling on a buffalo or other large mammal. It uses its curved bill to pick ticks off the animal's skin. It also warns the animal when danger approaches. In return for its hard work, the oxpecker gets a steady supply of tasty ticks!

CHAPTER 2

One-Sided Relationships?

Are there any animal partnerships in which one animal partner benefits and the other gets nothing in return? Most scientists think so. They call this type of relationship **commensalism** (kuh-MEN-suh-lih-zum). The relationship between the remora fish and the shark is an example of commensalism.

The remora have suction disks on their heads. They use the disks to attach themselves to the shark and go for a ride. When the shark kills its prey, the remora swim nearby, eating bits of leftovers. Most scientists believe the shark is neither helped nor harmed. Some scientists, however, say it's hard to prove that such relationships exist. They think the shark might be helped in ways we don't know about. For example, they think that the remora might help the shark by eating parasites off its body.

many remora attached to a shark

CHAPTER 3

Parasitism: Uninvited Guests

Parasitism is another type of partnership. In this relationship, one partner (the parasite) lives on or in the other partner's body (the **host**). This relationship benefits the parasite by providing it with food. The host is usually harmed in some way. In some cases, the harm is minor. In other cases, the parasite kills its host.

Mosquitoes

The female mosquito has sharp mouthparts to pierce its host's skin. It takes a female mosquito just two or three minutes to finish a meal of the host's blood.

Mosquitoes may carry dangerous viruses, such as the West Nile virus. These viruses can enter the hosts when mosquitoes attack.

It's a FACT

Only female mosquitoes are parasites. Male mosquitoes feed on nectar and plant juices.

A mosquito feeds on the blood from a human hand.

21

CHAPTER 3

They Made a Difference

In the early 1900s, work began on the Panama Canal in Central America. Many of the workers on the canal got sick and died from a virus known as yellow fever.

A U.S. Army doctor named Walter Reed proved that the yellow fever virus was carried by mosquitoes. Another army doctor named W. C. Gorgas set up a plan to control the number of mosquitoes along the canal route. Fewer mosquitoes meant less yellow fever.

Thanks to the efforts of Dr. Reed and Dr. Gorgas, the yellow fever virus was brought under control.

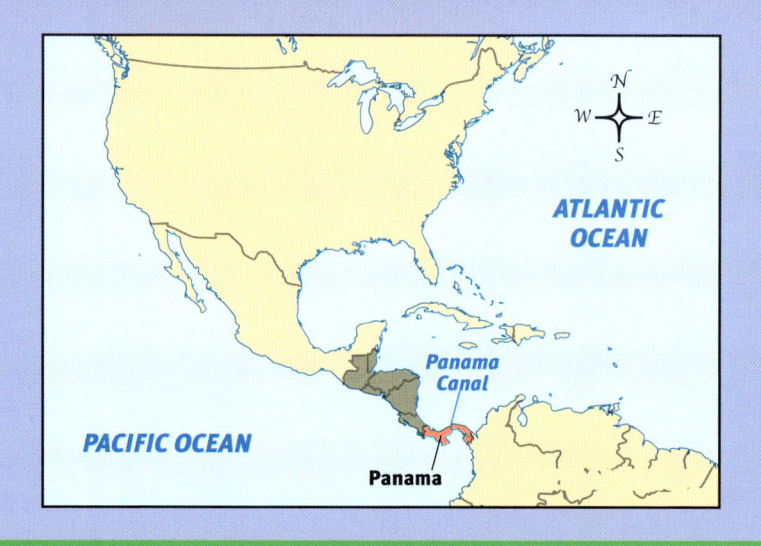

Dr. Walter Reed

PARASITISM: UNINVITED GUESTS

Deer Ticks

Deer ticks are parasites that feed on the blood of birds or mammals, such as deer, dogs, and humans. Deer ticks are so tiny that they're easy to miss. That's why many people bitten by them don't even realize it.

Some deer ticks carry Lyme disease, a serious bacterial infection. When ticks bite, they can pass on this disease to their victims.

In the late 1990s, scientists developed a vaccine for Lyme disease. Only time will tell whether the vaccine can help control the spread of this illness.

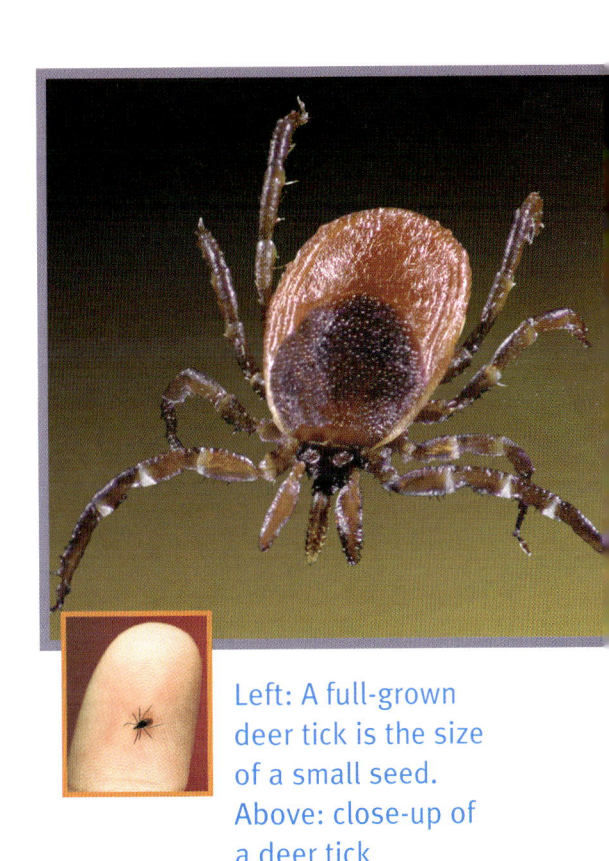

✓ Point

Make Connections
Have you learned how to avoid Lyme disease? When you're in the woods or grassy areas where deer ticks live, wear light-colored pants and long-sleeved shirts for protection. The light color makes it easier to see the ticks if they get on you. Tuck your shirt into your pants and your pants into your socks for extra protection.

Left: A full-grown deer tick is the size of a small seed. Above: close-up of a deer tick

CHAPTER 4

The Human Connection

two hunters with their prey on the Great Plains

Humans can play the roles of predator, prey, or host.

Humans as Predators

From our earliest days, humans have preyed on wild animals, such as buffalo, to survive. As time went on, humans began to raise animals such as cattle for food. Today, most of us don't kill the animals we eat. But we could still be considered predators when we buy meat to eat.

Humans have preyed on animals for reasons other than for food. In the 1800s, hunters killed millions of buffalo on the Great Plains, not just for their meat, but for their hides or just for sport. At one time, so many alligators were killed for their skins or for sport that they became rare. Today, alligators are no longer endangered.

24

Are humans considered predators in the following situations?

As the human population grows, we take over the habitats of many kinds of animals. What has happened to the animals that lived in those areas? In some cases, as with the grizzly bear, the populations have declined.

In other cases, marine animals, such as whales, dolphins, and manatees, have been injured or killed by people's boating activities.

In many places, wetlands have been drained for farming and building homes. This has caused the decline of animal populations, such as river otters and copperbelly snakes.

Building new homes means fewer animal habitats.

Science in the News

The news on December 24, 2003, was not good. The first case of mad cow disease had been discovered in the United States.

Cows infected with mad cow disease appear confused and clumsy. Eventually, they die. Scientists think that cows get the disease when they eat meal, or ground-up animal parts, made from diseased animals.

If people eat beef from infected cows, they can become infected, too. Experts think it could take up to ten years for the disease to show up in people who have been infected.

CHAPTER 4

Humans as Prey

Very rarely, humans can become prey of other animals. In some western states, humans are using or taking over the habitat of mountain lions. More people are living, hiking, camping, and biking in areas where mountain lions live. Although it doesn't happen often, the mountain lions sometimes attack. In January 2004, a man was killed by a mountain lion while biking in a California wilderness park. When he was found, his body had been half-eaten and was partly buried.

The same animal attacked, but did not kill, two young women later that same day. A deputy shot and killed the mountain lion involved in these attacks.

This hiker is in Olympic National Park, Washington.

THE HUMAN CONNECTION

It's a FACT

Mountain lions are known by many names—cougar, panther, puma, and catamount. They are among the largest wild cats in the Western Hemisphere. Mountain lions are very powerful. With their strong rear legs, they can leap about 15 feet in one jump.

Deserts, tropical jungles, and thick forests are all home to mountain lions. In the United States, they are most common in the Rocky Mountains and in states that border the Pacific Ocean.

Mountain lions usually prey on large animals like deer and elk, although they will hunt raccoons, rabbits, and other small animals. Normally, they stay away from people. Only about a dozen people have been killed by mountain lions in North America in the past 100 years.

CHAPTER 4

This photo has been enlarged to show human eyelashes and the tails of eyelash mites magnified x50. The eyelashes are shown in green. The tails of four eyelash mites are circled.

Humans as Hosts

As you read in Chapter 3, people can be hosts to parasites such as mosquitoes and ticks. If the mosquitoes or ticks that bite us are infected with a virus or bacteria, they can pass the disease on to us, their hosts. We then become prey to the virus or bacteria.

Humans are hosts to some parasites that cause no harm. For example, one harmless parasite is the eyelash mite. These tiny mites live in the pores on our faces and in the roots of our eyelashes. Eyelash mites feed on the fluids in our pores and the dead cells on our skin. We can't feel them, so we just try to pretend they aren't there!

In the following study, you will read about how humans can also be hosts to more harmful parasites.

28

THE HUMAN CONNECTION

Scientists investigated an illness at a college football game. Many players on the Duke University football team were not feeling well. As the game continued, eleven players from the other team also became sick. Epidemiologists traced the Duke players' illness to sandwiches they'd eaten. The sandwiches had been prepared by a food worker who had a virus.

How did the players who did not eat the sandwiches get sick? The scientists studied films of the game. They noticed that the sick Duke players wiped their mouthguards with their hands. They touched players from the other team during the game, and shook hands with them at the end. Further tests showed that players from both teams did indeed have the same virus.

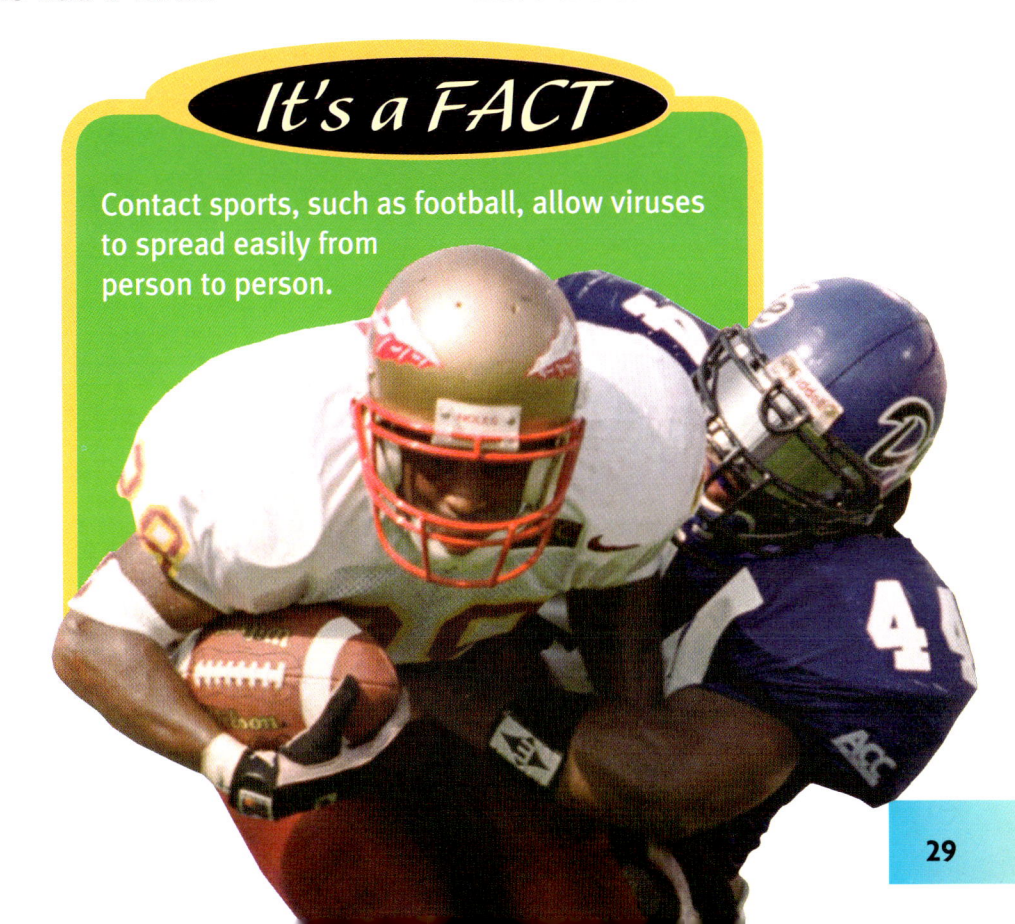

It's a FACT

Contact sports, such as football, allow viruses to spread easily from person to person.

Conclusion

Relationships among species vary. Some relationships are a fight to the finish between predator and prey. With mutualism, both partners benefit. In parasitic relationships, one partner may live on or inside the other, and usually causes harm.

There are many ways in which animals adapt to survive in nature. Predators have special abilities that help them hunt their prey. Prey have special abilities that help them escape their predators. And many animals are well suited to meet each other's needs.

Throughout history, humans have played the role of predator, prey, and host. Each of these roles has had a direct effect on other species. We need to think carefully about the human impact on other living things and act wisely. What we do today will influence the way we, and all living things, live tomorrow.

African buffalo and oxpecker

Glossary

adapt — (uh-DAPT) to adjust or change and thereby better survive in an environment (page 8)

camouflage — (KA-muh-flahj) a body coloring or pattern that helps an animal blend in with its surroundings (page 12)

commensalism — (kuh-MEN-sul-lih-zum) a relationship in which one animal benefits and the other is unaffected (page 20)

habitat — (HA-bih-tat) the native environment of an animal or plant (page 6)

host — (HOST) a living plant or animal on which a parasite lives (page 21)

mutualism — (MYOO-chuh-wuh-lih-zum) a partnership between two species in which both parties benefit (page 16)

parasitism — (PAIR-uh-sih-tih-zum) a relationship in which one organism benefits and the other is usually harmed (page 21)

predator — (PREH-duh-ter) an animal that hunts for its food (page 4)

prey — (PRAY) an animal that is hunted and killed for food (page 4)

scavenger — (SKA-ven-jer) an organism that eats the remains of dead animals (page 14)

species — (SPEE-sheez) a group of organisms that share the same characteristics (page 2)

Index

adapt, 8, 30

ant, 19

aphid, 19

apple snail, 6

camouflage, 12

cheetah, 2, 10, 14

clown fish, 2, 16–17

commensalism, 20

crow, 9

disease, 18, 28
    Lyme, 23
    mad cow, 25

epidemiologist, 29

habitat, 6, 25–26

honey badger, 18

honeyguide, 18

host, 21, 28, 30

human, 2–3, 23–24–26, 28, 30

hyena, 14

lynx, 4–5

mosquito, 2, 21–22, 28

mountain lion, 26–27

mutualism, 16, 18, 30

oxpecker, 19

parasite, 20–21, 23, 28

parasitism, 21

predator, 2, 4–10, 12–14, 16–17, 19, 24–25, 30

prey, 2, 4–16, 20, 24, 26–28, 30

remora, 20

scavenger, 14–15

shark, 20

snail kite, 6

snowshoe hare, 4–5

species, 2, 6, 9, 30

tick, 19, 23, 28

wrasse, 18